The Witch's Hut

by
Christopher Penczak

COPPER
CAULDRON
PUBLISHING

CREDITS

WRITING & ART: Christopher Penczak
EDITING: Tina Whittle
LAYOUT & DESIGN: Steve Kenson

Copyright ©2020 Christopher Penczak. All Rights Reserved. No part of this work may be reproduced, stored in a retrieval system, or transmitted in any form or by any means, without the express prior permission in writing of the Copyright Owner, nor be otherwise circulated in any form other than that in which it is published.

For more information, visit:
christopherpenczak.com
coppercauldronpublishing.com

ISBN 978-1-940755-12-0
First Edition, Printed in the U.S.A.

Special Thanks

...to Steve Kenson for his thoughtful feedback and insight into making this book a reality and to Tina Whittle for working her amazing magick upon the text.

Thanks to all the authors and teachers whose wisdom seeped into this story, including Laurie Cabot, Doreen Valiente, Dion Fortune, Starhawk, Raven Grimassi, Robert Cochrane, T. Thorn Coyle, Orion Foxwood, Michelle Belanger, Jan Brink, Adam Sartwell, Chris Giroux, Alix Wright, and Rosalie Penczak.

And deep gratitude to Mr. Day and Mr. Night, never the two shall meet.

Contents

I. Why?	1
II. The Common Sense of Nature	5
III. Blame	9
IV. Misfortune and Fate	13
V. The Soul	17
VI. Desire	21
VII. Omens	27
VIII. True Nature	31
IX. Mystery	35
X. Possession & Self-Possession	39
XI. Consequence	45
XII. Seasons	49
XIII. Are the Gods Real?	53
XIV. Justice	57
XV. Allies	61
XVI. Beauty	65
XVII. Domestication & Wildness	69
XVIII. Faith	73
XIX. The Unknown and Unknowable Mysteries	77
XX. Power	79
XXI. Love	83
XXII. Wisdom	87
Afterword	89

I.
Why?

The days shortened, and the skies darkened. Everyone grew colder. The land was dry, the harvest scarce. There had been much sickness and many deaths that year. Some old. Some young. It was a hard year for them all, and there was fear and sorrow in their hearts.

With the dark skies came the storms. With the storms came the pouring rain, the thunder and the howling wind. During one of these storms, lightning struck the thatched roof of a barn, catching it on fire. Despite the rains it burned, and what remained of the harvest was destroyed, ruined by fire and water. And this was the final act that broke them all.

"She did it!" one said. "You know she did."

"She's wicked," another responded. Soon a mob of wet and angry people had gathered in the dark, their frustrations mounting as one by one they added their anger and worry, their raw desperation, to the seething crowd.

She lived at the edge of the village, in her own hut. Everyone knew her. How could they not? She was everything separate from them. She took part only rarely in village life, keeping to herself, to her own strange ways. She would barter for some food, but mostly gathered her own. She would trade her medicines, sometimes offering a charm or two. She was willing to read the omens and give counsel. They in turn would give her a loaf of bread, some cheese, or the occasional coin. She was quite good at her work, though rarely popular, for unlike the soothsayers at the fairs and festivals, she told the truth, not what people wanted to hear.

In the past, she had been well admired. Everyone wanted to

be like her. Independent. Mysterious. Powerful. Wise. But their favor didn't last. Eventually people resented her. Why did she get to do whatever she wanted, while they could not? How was it that she could run with the creatures of the forest while they worked the fields? Why was she allowed to heed her own counsel, chief above all others? And so, sensing their growing resentment, she moved her hut further and further from the village.

With each distancing, she became more hideous to them. They remembered her in years past as captivating. Alluring. As age caught up with her, she seemed more gnarled, like the old trees she loved and tended. Elder-hood gave way to something else. At times it was as if she had stepped out of a children's tale. Sometimes she was the strange faery godmother, and at other times, perhaps, the monster.

Now the wet and angry crowd made its way along the path, over the stones and through the mud to her hut. They carried torches to provide light and shovels and pitchforks as makeshift walking sticks to guide them in the night. With single purpose, they moved as one towards her home. They grew into a mob.

She heard them coming. She saw their torches. She went to her door and said, "Why are you here? Why do you bother me on this night?"

"Our land will not produce food," said one. "We grow hungry."

Another spoke up. "Many people and animals have grown sick and died."

"Now the very heavens attack us with light and fire!" said a third. "We know that your sorcery, your wickedness, is to blame!"

And then they spoke as a mob. "Why have you done this to

us? Why have you cursed us so?"

She regarded them from her hut. The hearth fire flickering inside illuminated her presence, her silhouette framed by the sturdy beams of her threshold. "Why? You would ask me why? Listen, and I'll tell you why."

II.
The Common Sense of Nature

She put her hands on her hips. "Lightning strikes, yes, and it can lay waste. Yet the lightning brings renewal. There are many seeds in the forest that will not sprout without fire. The underbrush can choke out new life, and the fire spread by lightning clears the land. All things built up must be cut back to be regenerated, or they will overtake all and block out the light. We need both forests and fields."

"But why did it strike our barn?" one said.

"That is the nature of lightning. In the forest, it will often strike the tallest tree. In your village, the barn was the tallest thing, so naturally it struck there. I no more conjured it than I would call it to hit the great oaks of the forest. Don't assume malice or fantastic power where common sense will suffice."

She waved her hand to encompass the whole of the landscape. "The world is complex. How can we know anything for sure? There are so many possibilities. Yet our understandings can be simple. We can observe. We can see patterns. We can discern principles. We can learn. We add to our knowledge, yes, but more importantly, when we observe something intimately, we grow close with it, like an old friend. Only then will it slowly share its secrets with us. All of nature is a friend waiting for us to take the time to talk and to listen, but we must share our secrets with her.

"Nature follows her patterns. Nature sticks to her principles. Nature follows the path of least resistance. Nature takes the easy way. In her complexity, she is simple. Water flows and falls downward. Smoke rises. Winter becomes spring, then summer and fall. Eggs hatch. Berries ripen over time, and yes, lighting strikes from the heavens."

She examined the vine growing around her threshold, leafless now and dormant, and nodded to herself, satisfied that it remained intact after the storm. "Only when she knows us so deeply can we know her. Observations and understanding can only take us so far. Passive learning grows stale quickly. To receive we must give, and to give we must receive. We must love nature for her to love us back in this way. Her first gift of love was life itself, but when we love her, she lets us into her mystery. Only then can we remember."

III.
Blame

Backlit by the hearth fire inside, the Witch's shape cast shadows across them. Her voice carried in the still, deep darkness. "And yet you would blame me for these things? Why do you do this? I think that is a better question."

There was silence. They didn't know why, not really. They knew it was a bad reaction to the shock of the barn being struck by lightning. But there was something deeper still.

They didn't know why they blamed her, but blame her they did.

"Blame is like having something you no longer want," she said. "When given something that is unexpected, that shocks or hurts, our first thought is to foist it upon another. Like a hot potato burning our hands, we quickly pass it to another to deal with, rather than pause and take responsibility for it, perhaps even find a solution. But no, we try to give it back to whomever or whatever gave it to us in the first place. If the culprit is not obvious, we simply pick a convenient target to make the culprit. We pick someone who will not fight back or someone already blamed for other things, so that it will be as easy to convince people they are to blame as it was easy to convince ourselves. Or we pick someone we already blame for something else and make them the author of all our woes."

The villagers grew uneasy. They knew what it felt like to be blamed for something they hadn't done. They remembered being children in the world, and now with hungry children at their feet, they remembered even more strongly the piercing unfairness of it.

The Witch continued. "We feel that if we did not personally create it, we shouldn't be responsible for it. Yet we create many things we will not take credit for. Our words and actions, our very thoughts, have a long reach with results we don't always see or recognize, even when presented with them. We are all masterful magicians, but the difference is that I know this.

"There will be many results from the actions of others, from our ancestors, from the progress of nature, and from the stars themselves that reach us. We did not choose these results, but we must deal with these consequences anyway. If we take them personally, we seek to place blame, as we don't want to accept blame for something that is not our choice. If we choose to see them as part of the path of life, with its days and nights, summers and winters, we can choose wisely."

IV.
Misfortune and Fate

The rain continued to drizzle on them, but they couldn't stop listening. They stood as one, as if spellbound, their torches lower now, their shovels and pitchforks held loosely at their sides.

"If someone is not to blame, then why do we experience misfortune?" a woman asked. She had helped build the barn with her own two hands only to watch it collapse this night in sodden ash.

The Witch regarded the woman patiently. "Misfortune? Let me tell you why misfortune comes your way. Humans think their fortune is a wheel, turning like the wheel of the day, of the seasons. The wheel goes up, and we get what we want, or at least what we think we want. The wheel goes down, and an ill wind blows, and we have bad luck. We call it fortune, this random gaining or losing with the turn of the wheel. We call it a blessing or a curse of birth, and ponder how some seem lucky while others are not. We go through periods of good or ill, and the wheel turns again."

She shook her head. "What men call fortune, I call fate. But fate is not what is destined to happen without fail. Fate is no decree from the gods. Fate is what is most likely to happen given everything that has happened before, everything that has led to this moment. You can change your fate by changing your actions, your words, and your thoughts. You might have to fight the momentum of those thoughts, words, and actions, and the momentum of those who have acted before you, but each time you choose your own fate, you turn the wheel once again. My spells, my rituals, are all a means to help turn the wheel of Lady Fate, but they are just tools. My goal is not good luck."

A boy stepped forward. He was dressed in tattered rags. Behind him stood his father, one of the first to rouse the mob. "Why not?" he asked. "Everyone wants to be lucky! Everyone wants to get what they want, don't they?"

The Witch nodded. "Yes, everyone might want that when they start. But after enough times of not getting what you want and being thankful in hindsight, or getting something better than your short-sighted desire, you start to desire what you need, even if you don't know what that is."

The boy stared, silent. His father put a hand on his shoulder, but did not pull him back. He let the boy stand and listen, just as he himself now listened.

The Witch continued. "Rituals and spells help us orient on the wheel of fortune we all walk. Most walk on the rim. When they are on top, they feel lucky, unbeatable. When they fall to the bottom, they feel like a failure and can't think of anything but reaching the top again. Why? Do we fail when winter comes? Do we succeed by the virtue of the summer? Does dawn come to bless us and night come to punish us? No. Of course not. Why is it that fate is not a part of nature as well, for she is like a sister to nature?

"The secret of the wise is to learn to be free from fate. We learn to not only turn the wheel again, but to find the part of us that exists in the center of the wheel, that observes all our rising and falling, but does neither. We find the part of ourselves that walks the spokes of the wheel, communicating between the center and rim. With this knowledge we understand the nature of the soul."

V.
The Soul

"The soul?" the woman cried out. She pushed to the front of the crowd. "What does the soul have to do with the lightning and the burning barn? How does this help us?"

The Witch spoke calmly, her words carrying in the damp night air. "A barn is like your body. It will pass. It will grow old, and no matter how much you repair it, eventually it will fail you. But the soul will continue, just not in the way you think.

"Beware those who seek to control your soul. Beware those who tell you that you have only one. They seek to use hope and fear to control your body by convincing you they can control the destiny of your soul. But they can no more control the soul after death than they can change the course of the stars on a whim."

An older man, one of the more learned in the village, said, "Of course we only have one soul. Who told you we have more?"

"The wise have always known we have more than one soul," she replied. "There is more than one you, isn't there? 'You' is a collective of many little selves with different points of view. Each is a soul. And each soul will be true to its nature upon death. No one can control it."

She gestured to the sky above, dark still and clotted with clouds. "You have a soul that sits in the center of the wheel. This is the soul of the stars, belonging above. You have always been a little light that shines in the darkness of space. This soul is never born. This soul never dies. This soul is timeless."

She gestured to the crowd itself. "You have a soul that walks the rim of the wheel. This soul sees itself as you, as human. This soul knows your name. This soul knows your face. This one experiences the ups and downs of life, the desires and disappointments."

She dug the tip of her shoe into the wet earth at her feet, rich and smelling of rain. "You have a soul that dreams deeply, that remembers the world before there were humans upon it. This soul walks the spokes of the wheel and digs deep within the land and digs deep in our bodies. This soul moves us to fight or flee, to play, to dance, and to sing. This soul has no pretense. It simply feels and acts upon its instincts.

"Our job is to have the three souls act as one. Our task in this life is to learn to desire what our souls desire collectively for us and then make it happen."

VI.
Desire

The crowd murmured uneasily. This sounded of heresy to them. Dangerous. Even more dangerous than lightning.

The Witch noticed their discomfort. "Desire is holy. Do you know this? Most people don't. We are not taught to desire things. But the act of wanting is holy, for yearning points us towards our souls.

"We don't always get what we desire, and that is holy too.

"When we desire something, we are recognizing where we feel incomplete or unsatisfied as we are. Sometimes we look to things outsides of ourselves for satisfaction, but nothing outside of us will satisfy us. Things outside of us embody what we feel we lack, or things we have not yet experienced. When we obtain what we lack, and we are satisfied, we experience a shift within, a step towards better understanding of our own completeness."

The crowd was unconvinced. How could this be true? In times of want and need, how could that aching emptiness be holy?

The Witch continued. "Sometimes we obtain what we desire, but we are not satisfied. Sometimes it is not what we expected or hoped for, or only an outer form that fails to speak to our souls. Once we discover it is empty, we can move on and let it go. Continuing to desire it would be a great distraction from our own journey."

The villagers listened. Deep in their hearts, they knew this feeling of dissatisfaction and the resentment that came with it. Was that not ingratitude? What was the difference? They gripped their torches more tightly, their tools as well, their fingers closing almost involuntarily on the worn, familiar objects.

The Witch took note of this, calmly. "Sometimes we get what we asked for, but not what we thought we were asking for. We were unclear in our heart and mind, and unclear in our thoughts, words, and actions. We must seek clarity before trying to fulfill any dreams or desires.

"When we fail to obtain what we want, we should ask why. Sometimes we didn't put any effort into it. Sometimes we are unclear in our hearts and minds. Sometimes our want is in conflict with our souls, and our souls orchestrate life events to prevent that desire from manifesting."

The learned man shook his head, his voice rising against the rain. "That doesn't make any sense. Why would we want something our soul doesn't?"

The Witch regarded him knowingly. "Why? Because we are self-deceptive, self-destructive creatures. We fail to listen to our true inner yearnings and try to emulate the goals and desires around us. When someone has something we do not possess, we want it, even if we don't need it or have never wanted it before. Jealousy arises. Rather than be happy for another, we see their happiness as sign of our lack, and rather than find our own way, we try to take what is theirs, assuming it is the source of their happiness."

The man's forehead creased. "Are you accusing us of stealing?"

The Witch shook her head patiently. "No, I'm not. We live in a world that tells us what success or happiness is, and we try to capture it, but each of our souls has its own vision of success, happiness, and true purpose. Desire is holy because pursuing desire helps us examine and discard those ideas and expectations that come from outside of us, to find the will of the deepest soul from within.

"When our strongest desire is to fulfill the will of the deepest soul, we have found the way. At first we might desire it, but have no knowledge of what the soul wants at all. Our three souls working as one gives us our true purpose in this lifetime, and once we want to fulfill it, we must go on a journey to discover it."

The young boy piped up again. "Journey? Where? My mother won't let me leave the village."

She smiled at him. The young were always closer to the truth than they knew.

"Wise men say 'follow your bliss,' and they are half right," she said. "Following your soul is blissful in so many ways, but like anything, it is also hard work. It is also trial and error. It is also dealing with people who are not in their bliss. For every rose, there is a stem full of thorns. Life does not become perfect once you decide to follow your bliss. But that which brings you true joy can be a key to understanding the way. Remember, that which you think will bring you joy will not always be joyful, and the path of your bliss might lead you in a direction you have never considered. Do you think I always wanted to live at the edge of the village? Did you think I wanted this role I have taken? Do you think anyone wants to be the dark mirror?"

This baffled them. She was asking them a question they had never considered. The Witch had desires? Needs? Unfulfilled wishes and tribulations?

"What did you want?" someone asked from the back of the crowd.

The Witch pondered the question seriously. "I had very ordinary dreams. I dreamed of marriage. Children. I dreamed the dreams of my mother and father. I watched my sisters and brothers. I never dreamed my path would turn. But it did, and while I am not always happy, I am blissful."

They thought on this word. Blissful. Didn't that mean the same thing as happy?

"What's the difference?" another person asked.

"To find the path of your soul, what brings you true joy opens the way. But it is not easy. Every day is a quest thrashing about in the thicket, on the thorny path. No one will cut your path out for you. They will barely cut their own. You must be the one to make your own path by walking it. The well-worn path comes from walking it.

"As we continue, we look for the world to show us the way. We look to the Soul of the World to guide us. We listen and learn. We seek portents and omens to show us."

VII.
Omens

The villagers were silent. What was she talking about? Portents and omens? Those were things of her world, not theirs. That was why they kept each to their own ways, separate from her.

A young girl released her mother's hand and stepped forward, closer than any of them had dared, close enough to touch the old woman if she had wanted.

"The world has a soul?" she said in a half-whisper.

The Witch looked the child in the eye. "Yes. When we seek on this quest, the Soul of the World speaks to us. She wants us to succeed as much as we want to succeed, or even more. For she is a part of us, and we are a part of her.

"When we speak, she listens. When we ask questions, she offers answers, but we need to have the ears to hear and the eyes to see to understand those answers. While many see and hear clearly, few perceive truly. Many of those who do truly perceive are considered blind or deaf by the masses. So she has taught us new ways to speak and listen."

"Like what?" the child said.

"The events of our future, our likely fate, cast shadows backwards in time just as our actions cast ripples forward in time. To read the omens is to read the patterns of light and shadow here and now to find the future. We can use them to change course or find assuredness to stay the course we follow.

"We look to the omens in nature. We see the future in the

flight of birds, in the trees, and in which animals cross our path. And we see the omens in the stars and in the cards, in the bones and stones, even in the lines on our hands.

"Everything is speaking. Everything is teaching. Everything wants to aid you on the quest if you'll but listen."

The child's mother stepped forward. She stood behind her daughter, her hands on the thin, slight shoulders. "But how do you know?" she said. "How do you know what you hear and see is the truth?"

VIII.
True Nature

The question hung in the wet night air, heavy and ponderous.

The Witch knew the mother. She had been widowed very young, and having worked the family farm alone for many years she was strong, good with beasts of all kinds. She reminded the Witch of her own younger self, quick of tongue and sharp of eye. Not a woman who approved of mobs, and yet, there she was in the middle of this one.

"When you listen to nature," the Witch said, "when you see the signs, you begin to also know yourself. You are a part of nature. Just as the seed knows how to sprout and the Sun knows how to rise, you know how to do your will. Yet for some reason, humans are the only part of nature that likes to forget. Perhaps it's because we also fully partake in the game of fate. Perhaps not. Yet we seem to be able to fully choose, and we often choose poorly for ourselves and for others."

A smoke-gray feline appeared at her ankles. It sat itself on the ground at her feet, its tail switching back and forth. Its yellow eyes blinked, and the firelight tinged its silhouette with a golden glow. It looked up at her and meowed.

The Witch bent to pick it up. "When we start to listen to our own nature, we become true to our nature. Yet in that truth there are traps. There is a reason why we have choice. Without it, we might be slaves to our routines and take the easy path. We might never aspire. We might never ask why. Yet we shouldn't seek to be anything other than who we are. A duck doesn't try to be a horse. A spider doesn't seek to be a rock. Everything grows to its own nature, in its own time and way. Everything grows towards its own perfection."

A night bird called from the forest, and the cat leaped from her arms and disappeared into the darkness, graceful and swift. The Witch did not seek to catch it or call it back, and the villagers watched it blend with the shadows and vanish, as if it were a wisp of smoke.

"So we must be true to our nature, but not trapped by our nature," the Witch said. "Follow your instincts, your essence, but never stop seeking. Where nature and fate dwell together, we find the Soul of the World. And in the Soul of the World, all things are possible."

A young man shouldered his way through the crowd until he stood in front of the old woman. "We must seek, you say? As if we aren't always seeking already, always on the lookout for the next scrap of food, the next piece of firewood. The next hole in the roof, the next sickness too. Life is one endless seeking after another."

She was not offended, even though the young man's words were laced with bitterness. She knew his family, knew the reasons behind his anger, for his mother had visited her many times in the darkest hours of the night.

"We have inherent patterns," said the Witch. "No one needs to tell us how to grow up, or how to grow old. We invest no thought in breathing or digestion. It just happens. Yet we know we are on the wheel, that a part of us is on the wheel, going up and going down, and we want to control that. We want to understand. Most creatures simply go with the flow of the wheel. They don't seek control. They don't seek to know why. Our desire to know why things are the way they are, to know who we are and what we are here to do, separates us from those who have no questions of their purpose and no questions of the world. Our seeking and yearning open the gates to the Mysteries."

IX.
Mystery

The young man frowned. "Mysteries? What mysteries?"

By this time, all sense of threat to the old woman had ended. Their shovels and pitchforks were still, no longer brandished about. The people leaned on them as if they were walking sticks. The torches were extinguished in the rain, but the blazing fire in her hearth provided light to see. Many had sat down in the mud or upon stumps to listen, as if she were a grand storyteller at their campfire.

They were entranced by her words. She had cast no spell that they could see, but they could not deny that magick was flowing. Something was happening. They were being led somewhere, but they knew not where. The magick hung in the air, palpable, like the breath of some great old beast, yet no one was afraid anymore.

"What are the Mysteries indeed!" the lady of the hut responded. "If we knew, then they wouldn't rightly be called Mysteries, would they?"

"If we can't know them, what good are they? Mysteries don't put food on my table," said a farmer, one of the more successful ones in the village. He had stayed at the edge of the crowd all night, as if he were unsure of his place there, but now his voice rang clear.

The Witch drew to her full height. "I beg to differ. The greatest of Mysteries puts food on the table. What is the growth of the grain but a mystery? What is the sprouting of a seed, but a mystery? What is the birth and life of an animal, but a mystery? We may have explanations of how it happens, but it doesn't tell us why.

"The tides of life and death that rule us are a mystery. The tides of light and dark governing our land are a mystery. There are things to be discovered in life and in death. We must ask ourselves the sacred questions:

"Who Am I?"

"What Am I?"

"Where are we?"

"When is it?"

"How did this happen?"

"Why—and what's next?"

"The Mysteries are only known through the asking, and through experience. There is no one right answer for us all. Through nature, through our omens, we find our eyes that can see and our ears that can hear. We ask and we wait, but in the waiting we experience what life has to offer, and it is in the experience we find the answer to our Mysteries. Living life is the greatest mystery of all, until we face the next; the mystery of death."

The people felt a mutual shiver run through them. In their minds, one did not name such things so lightly. One did not speak that word so easily. And yet here she was, letting even that greatest of troubles fall from her lips. They knew death intimately, knew enough to not call its name aloud. But the spell, the magick, kept them listening.

The witch continued, her voice even stronger now, resonating through the clearing. "Our people saw themselves in the world. The growth cycle of the crops, the hunt, the turning of the Sun, Moon, and stars, these are all ways of seeking the Mysteries. War, motherhood, the gods, illness, sex, emotion, and the mind are all gates to the Mysteries. Everything is a door. Everything hides a teacher."

"The Mysteries help us find our place within, and our place without. Like a compass, we are oriented in both the inner worlds and the outer worlds through our family, friends, and community. We learn where we are all together in the great cycle of history. We tell stories to explain how and why everything happened, and they are all true, for us. And none of them are true. The Mysteries are found in paradox, where everything is true and nothing is true, and meaning is what you make of it. Everything is held in potential. That is the secret to magick. The experience of the Mysteries leads you to self-possession."

X.
Possession & Self-Possession

"I don't want to be possessed!" cried someone from the crowd, and other voices echoed the cry.

The woman regarded them with a level gaze. She didn't answer immediately; she simply turned around and faced the door of her hut. Reaching inside the frame, she grabbed a brown leather pouch dangling from a rawhide cord.

The crowd murmured amongst themselves. What strange things were hidden within that bag? What was she going to do with it?

Dangling the pouch from her hands, she turned her attention once again to the crowd. "Do you fear a ghost or demon will grab hold of your body? That a night-mare will ride you in the dream word until exhaustion? That is what we have been taught, and it is true. There are forces that would take control of us and command us against our will and many of those forces are spirits, but I'd be more afraid of the ones you can see right before you. I'm more afraid about men who coerce us to do their bidding, and we do so because we are told to do it. They use fear, shame, and our own anger and prejudice against us. They call it duty, and honor, and patriotism. They mesmerize and convince us, and in doing so, they lead us into the unspeakable. They mesmerize and convince us. We agree, and we allow them to do it. When we agree to the evil of men, they cast the spell that is hardest to break."

The bag swung from her fingers, back and forth, as she spoke of evil and spirits and forces beyond their ken. Yes, they knew there was evil beyond the edge of their village. But they also knew there was evil among them, lurking in some hearts like a fester.

The firelight flickered behind the Witch as she stood in the threshold. "On some level, be it the darkest demon or the vilest tyrant, we allow them into the shrine of our souls. We open the door. Sometimes we even give them a key and set them a plate. While we may not always control the outer circumstances, we can live under tyranny and resist. We are not possessed. But when we give in to it, we become like tyrants, at least for a time.

"Magick is in our thoughts, words, and deeds, and it is through these things they come in. Many of the demons are parasites, simple beasts feeding off our unhealthy thoughts and magnifying our bad choices to create more food for themselves. We become their livestock, yet they are not farmers or shepherds."

The forest seemed to grow denser around them. They felt as if it were pressing in, as if hungry throats waited just beyond the circle of the clearing, as if the woods were a live thing, singular and ravenous.

The Witch lowered her voice. "Many demons are the whispering ones, the chattering ones, the howling ones. As the angels correspond to the virtues of creation, these creatures parallel our faults. They are drawn to us when our inner voice grows dark. They are found in our gossip and our sharp tongues. They are found in our willingness to go along with harm.

"Those of the wise learn the tenet 'As Above so Below' along with 'As Within, so Without.' It is the wisdom of correspondence and a great secret to magick. Everything in the heavens is reflected in the world. Everything outside of us has its reflection inside of us. All things we consider good and all things we consider bad have their reflections.

"When they possess us, they hold us, like I'm holding this." She held up the bag so that they could see it. "They use us. They own us. That is what we consider possession, ownership. We can hold something and do what we want with it. They treat us like we treat our possessions. We are eventually forgotten and discarded for more interesting toys."

To a person, they could not look away. Fingers felt again for the comfort of wooden handles and sharp blades, things to keep back the night.

The Witch saw, and felt no threat. She knew it meant that they had been paying attention.

She continued speaking. "But I ask you, can we possess anything? Do we truly own anything? The first thing we get on this journey is our body, and it's the last thing we give up. Despite our ancestors' burials with grave goods and other treasures, we can't take it with us, so do we really own it at all?

"Those on the path of mystery eventually realize we own nothing. Nothing! When walking with spirit, everything is on loan from nature, including our body. Everything is on loan from the Soul of the World, even our identity. We must give it all back. But one on the path has use of everything, for she knows she owns nothing.

"Fear not possession. For possession and self-possession are very different things. The only thing that truly belongs to us is ourselves. It is the only real method of protection from possession. Know thyself and belong to thyself, to the 'you' beyond body, thoughts, and identity."

Rummaging around her leather bag, she pulled out a berry-sized pearl and held it up, showing the crowd.

"Our true nature is like this pearl; beautiful and otherworldly.

The pearl has its own shape but reflects all upon its surface. The bag is who I think I am. It's all the things, good and bad, I've accumulated in my life. The bag seeks the pearl. Yet inside the bag, even with a little light, the pearl can only reflect the contents of the bag.

"When we are self-possessed, we bring more of the pearl into our conscious awareness. We generate the light within and can see ourselves as we truly are. When we start acting as if we are the pearl, not the bag, we make better choices.

"For those of us clearly on the wheel of fate, the pearl is with the self in the center of the wheel. The bag is with the self on the rim of the wheel, going up and down. When we live from the pearl, the two are one. We are on the edge and we are in the center at the same time. We are self-possessed, and nothing and no one can possess us again. The pearl will reflect and reveal what is not us, and we easily shake off their spell."

XI.
Consequence

The Witch returned the pearl to the bag. "There is consequence to all that we do. And while we might not be to blame for our circumstances, we are responsible. We have to take action and respond to all that we experience."

A woman from the back of the crowd stepped forward, and the people moved aside to make a path for her. She was almost as old as the woman in the hut and carried nothing except an ancient walking stick, weathered yet still solid. 'That doesn't make any sense. If I didn't do it, why do I have to fix it? If it's not my fault, why do I have to take action? I have enough problems."

The Witch nodded in agreement. "Yes, that would be wonderful, would it? Only taking care of yourself? Only doing what you want, what makes you happy? I would love to live in that world.

"For instance, in that world, like in this world, the lightning wasn't my fault. So you all showing up at the door to my hut, seeking to hurt me or kill me in revenge, is also not my fault or my responsibility. You should have simply left me alone. But you didn't, so here we are. Thankfully you listened before attacking. Luckily, I was able to hold your attention."

Everyone got very quiet and looked down sheepishly, their feet scuffling the ground. She let them do this just long enough for the discomfort to seep in deep, so that they would remember the feeling the next time misfortune struck their village. When she spoke, her voice was not accusatory. It was almost gentle.

"We are all here together upon the Earth," she said. "Some of us get along. Some less so. Many have chosen community. Others have not. But we all continue to cross paths whether we choose to or not. Our curiosity, our sense of adventure, our desire not to be bored ushers us outward to experience life. We experience not just other people, but animals, plants, and all of nature simply because we go out the door and into the world. We are sharing this time and place by the virtue of our existence, whether we like it or not. We can't escape that, so we shouldn't try. There is wisdom to be gained by dealing with it as it is.

"While I might not personally be the cause of something, if it ends up on my doorstep, in my life, it becomes a part of my work. The person who caused it could be dead. Or perhaps they have abdicated responsibility because it didn't have personal consequences. If it does for me, and I can't get the person who caused the trouble to do anything about it, I have to do something if I desire it to change. Who else will? If everyone says it's not their problem, then nothing gets solved."

The woman wrapped her shawl more tightly around her shoulders, her eyes flashing in outrage. "The world is running over with problems. Problems here, problems there. Awash in problems. How am I supposed to fix them all?"

The Witch shook her head. "You cannot be responsible for everything. So be responsible for your own personal nation, your own life, wherever that takes you. You are sovereign. That doesn't mean, despite mad queens and kings, that you can do whatever you like. It means you take responsibility for the realm, even cleaning up the mistakes of a past or neighboring king. Be responsible for what shows up before you as much as you can."

"How are we supposed to do that?" the woman replied. Her expression remained skeptical.

The Witch explained. "Consequence is ruled by both intention and perception, but neither of these shield you from its results. Intention can sow the seeds of future consequence, but if your intention is noble and your follow-through is poor, even the best of intentions can create misery and harm. Still, the worst of intentions almost always leads to misery and harm, so we must start with good—and clear—intent. That can guide us as well any anything or anyone.

"Perception allows you to change your relationship with a consequence even if its basic nature and end result haven't changed. See it differently, interact with it differently, and your experience will be different. An illness can be a villain coming to kill you, or a teacher trying to show you. Either way you die, but did you die in fear or in learning? A wise one knows the power of naming, how to transform things by what they are called. That which you look at looks back at you.

"One who is self-possessed moves through life accepting what is before them as part of the path, as the raw materials to craft our life. One who is not self-possessed gets the same thing, but walks through life without knowing it and has less power to change it."

XII.
Seasons

The Witch held up her hand, catching a few final raindrops in her open palm. The sky was dark still, thick with clouds, but the rain was beginning to lessen. She noted this as she noted the wind dying down too, still high in the treetops but no longer fierce.

"We walk through life marking patterns and seasons," she said. "We start like a seed, in darkness. We come forth into the light with water and blood, almost unrecognizable. We slowly mature and unfold. We experience the spring of our lives and our youth. Growth is the hallmark of this season. Everything is new. We flower and draw beauty. Even those who do not show a beautiful flower still blossom in some way. We have the grasses and the catkins of trees. Not everyone is a lily or rose, but some of the most beautiful flowers are weeds, for they thrive in the harsh conditions where no one wants them, usurping the territory of the approved plants."

The villagers remembered spring. The burst and blossom, the exuberance and promise. The tender mornings and freshening breezes and the growing light, each day like new cloth being woven on the loom.

"Summer brings maturity," the Witch said. "We ripen. We bear our own seeds and fruits and even nuts. Some find the summer harvest in their family. Others in their work and art. But the promise of the flower bears out. Or it doesn't. Not all plants yield a crop. The heat brings an intensity. There is a seriousness to it. We know even as we hit the peak of light and life that there will be a decline. Overhanging the summer is the dog star Sirius, marking the heat. And in our own dog days of life, the promise of Sirius, of the sacred, hangs over us. No time to lose."

She said the last words with a seriousness, and the villagers felt the heat in their bones, and the impetus that came with it. Those days were long, but each one shorter, each one pointing the way inexorably forward.

"Time takes its toll as we enter into autumn," she said. "Time hangs over us with its sickle. For the harvest is complete now. What was brought into manifestation is now released. The grain is cut. The fruit is picked. The herd is slaughtered and salted or smoked. All is in decline in our life. We think our usefulness has ended. We have given our all. And in return? In return we receive all, in the gift of the mystery."

The villagers remembered the autumn, the balefires and the turning leaves, the scent of ashes and the crispness of apples. The light grew clearer, the shadows darker, until night and day were equal, and then the night grew longer and darker still.

"By winter we are done," she said. "But in the mystery of the root, we may return again. The roots hold memory. The roots hold wisdom. The roots nourish and love us. The roots hold power, the power to sleep and dream. We return to darkness and shall rise again as we did like the first time when we began as a seed."

She saw the villagers nodding at this. They remembered the ground, hard as granite, and the sky, cold as the bottom of a well. But the roots survived. Every spring, there was rebirth and regeneration, greening and softening and newness. Could what she was saying be true? Could they be of the same pattern as the flowers and the trees, the seeds and the roots?

XIII.
Are the Gods Real?

An older boy, one the village would say was almost a man, looked up at the Witch. "The minister says this is the work of God and that we shouldn't ask questions. He said we must submit."

The Witch regarded him. "God? Have I said anything about God? No, I haven't."

The boy frowned. "You don't believe God is real?"

"Before you can ask, 'Is God real?', you have to answer, 'What is God?' And even, 'What is real?' We would like to think there is someone in charge, responsible for everything. That way, when things go wrong for us, we have someone to ask, or someone to blame when there is no answer. Tell me, child, who is in charge of your household?"

"My father," the boy replied.

"Is he really? Your father can guide, lead, or even force, ruling through love, fear, or guilt, but there is always something out of his control. Your unseen actions affect your siblings, your entire family. There is always another family, another father, another chief, another land that changes his outcome, beyond his control. So if your father cannot control your household, how can any god control everything?

"Perhaps there is no one God, but instead many gods, like there are many households. Some are guided by a father, others by a mother. Some are led by sisters or brothers or any others you can imagine. They are all gods. They all have a role to play, and on one level, they are all part of the greater world. On another they can get along like neighbors one day, and clash like neighbors the next. When they do, our world shifts. Sometimes it's for the better for us, and sometimes for the worse. Those actions ripple out, but they do not control the final result. The chaos and confusion are many forces working at once. If there is any "one God," the one is the container to hold the many."

The people murmured amongst themselves. This sounded of sacrilege. And yet, there was reason in it.

The Witch saw their struggle. "We know things are out of our control, so we want to be assured someone, anyone, is in control. When we get sick, we want to get better. When we don't get better, or when a loved one doesn't, we want to lash out when we realize we are not always in control. Life and death are not up to us. We can lose those we love and often think it unfair. Why do people have to die? We forget we are like the seeds. We have our cycle, or circle. Death, like birth, is the most personal thing we can experience, but it is also completely impersonal. It happens to everyone.

"We experience gain and good fortune, and we praise the gods. We experience loss and illness, and we blame the gods. But is there anything to praise and blame?" She shrugged. "Who knows? Many swear there is one God for that is all they know and believe. Others have known the gods of their ancestors, and see a world filled with gods. Others have no evidence of their reality and dismiss any possibility. The reality of the gods depends on your point of view. Everywhere we stand, things look different. We cannot measure the gods as we measure ourselves, yet we see many things as visible signs of their passing."

The sky was dark and complete around them. Lightning flared at the far horizon, silent and distant, a memory now. There was no longer the smell of smoke in the air, only the heavy ponderous scent of wet earth and storm-lashed vegetation.

"God is a mystery that you can only answer for yourself, and you might find the answer changes over time," said the Witch. "As soon as you think you have the answer for anyone else, you have lost the question. You can only seek the mystery for yourself and your way may or may not point the way for others. Some say we are born to learn to become gods, yet if that is true..." She smiled ruefully, gently. "We have a lot left to learn."

XIV.
Justice

The old farmer was not pleased. "Of course God exists. Without God, how can we have any justice?"

"What does one have to do with the other?" the Witch answered. "It's like asking 'how can we have cheese if we cannot fly to the Moon?' Our stories might say the Moon is made of cheese, but in truth it's not. We don't get cheese from the Moon. Likewise, our myths might say the gods mete out justice, rewarding the good and punishing the bad, yet that doesn't appear to be the way the world works. Many wonderful people suffer for things over which they have no control, and many wicked people thrive, at least for a time. You know this is true. So I ask you, what is justice?"

The man remained stubborn. "Adherence to the law and punishment when you do not."

"No, justice is not reward and punishment, but rather a force of balance. There is human justice and natural justice, but it is better to think of them as adjustment and equilibrium. Equilibrium can be met, but it's never static. Just when one level is balanced, something else shifts. Nature is an elder to us, and her life is much longer. Her need for balance is not as quick as ours, in our short lives. Humans try to emulate nature, but we speed it up to our time frame. We make rules and laws, seeking to create stability and harmony in our short lives. We want to reward the good and punish the evil, yet we all think we are good, and we are all still in conflict. Very few think they are truly evil, and those who do are simply hurt by others. Those who do the most harm feel completely justified in their actions, and expect to be rewarded for their cleverness, daring, or passion. None of our laws can cover every situation, but we try. We make more and more rules and laws in an effort to be just, and create more and more holes, allowing people to circumvent justice and yet feel they are doing good because they followed the letter of the rules, but not their spirit. The simplest of rules is best, but that leaves a wide range of interpretations, creating the desire for more clarity, more rules."

The farmer did not say anything. He knew this to be true, for he himself had argued for more laws, stricter laws, better laws. Justice was a solid, unbending structure, he had often said, with walls of thick stone. Now, as the old woman in the hut spoke, he realized that his vision looked very much like a prison.

The Witch continued. "We hope for someone or something wiser than us, to make the rules and mete out justice. We cling to ideas of justice, and even think they come from a god, but they are always through the lips and hands of humans, no matter how well intentioned. We seek to bind the destruction and wars directed to us by our concept of justice, but justice is only found when we are all seeking balance ourselves, and that balance is never set. We must constantly adjust."

XV.
Allies

The farmer crossed his arms. "And how exactly are we supposed to find this balance?"

"Some seek balance through solitude," the Witch replied. "They go alone. They shun the world and the company of others, going completely within. This can work for a time, but the true test of balance is how one acts around others. All the philosophy and insight in the world won't save you when a child is hungry, your loved one is ill, or another attacks you. If you don't challenge your ideas of balance and harmony, your wisdoms, to see if they work in the world, you'll never know.

"Others seek balance in community. They look to those close to them for help and support. They form relationships and groups with others for mutual aid. They start with families, then expand to friends, and then some seek a family of the chosen, those of like mind and similar interests, to support their quest. Most don't even know they are seeking balance. They seek happiness. They seek success. Some seek fame or power. But all are moving in small and large ways towards their vision of balance, testing it as they engage with the world."

The farmer grew silent again. He had never married, had never had a family. He had poured his time and attention into his land, his livestock, his home, the things he could keep in fences and behind hedgerows.

As the Witch spoke, the gray cat returned from the garden, a fat mouse in its jaws. The cat loped past the open doorway and behind the wood pile. Sleek as a shadow, she vanished into that particular darkness.

The Witch followed the animal with her eyes. "Along with our world of flesh and blood and form, all creatures seek their balance, including those in the world of spirit and twilight. Humans, animals, and even plants and stones are not alone in the world. Along with the spirits of the mountains and rivers, lakes and forests, deserts and prairies, are the spirits between."

The young girl who had spoken previously had been silent for a long time, but now her eyes grew wide. "Spirits?"

"Yes. The ancestors of all those who have gone before us, human and otherwise, dwell all around us. Invisible allies they are, along with other races who have never lived in flesh. Faeries, elves, sprites, specters, and angels all walk with us.

"By calling to those who dwell unseen around us for aid, we also aid them. We form relationships. Sometimes our agreements are informal, like friends. Others grow over time. Some are formalized contracts and ritualized agreements. The service is mutual. We learn more about their world. They learn more about ours. We work together to find balance between the worlds. Our gratitude for their help is mirrored by their gratitude towards us."

"How do you know these things?" the girl asked.

"Because this is what we Witches do the most. We engage with the unseen in kinship and gratitude. Our rituals, or spells, engage and entice these relationships, fostering the powers to communicate with them, aiding them and ourselves. We call to the spirits of the herbs and stones. We call to the spirits of the hills and trees. We call to the elves and angels, to the gods who walked before. But so do you. The ancestors dwell in your blood and whisper to you. The animals and plants you consume become one with you. The minerals and stones are within your body and bones. We Witches simply use ritual to make our wishes and actions clear to the unseen. Whether you seek or fear the Witch in her hut at the edge of the village, that is what we do.

"The two most powerful rituals any of us can engage in are service and gratitude. To be thankful for what is opens your heart to the deep magick of the world. To be of service to another, seen or unseen, can generate gratitude throughout the world, opening other hearts and minds. Use these rituals often and wisely."

XVI.
Beauty

The girl tilted her head back until she was looking the Witch directly in the eye. "Can the spirits make me beautiful?"

The Witch smiled. "What a question. Do you find me beautiful?"

The girl didn't answer, but everyone else looked away, for in truth the Witch was not fair to behold. She wasn't as monstrous as they'd imagined, though. When examined without fear, she was exactly average, but she radiated a magnetic wildness that drew those seeking something true. It wasn't beauty in the classic sense, but it was mesmerizing.

She saw the reaction of the crowd, but instead of being offended, she seemed almost amused. "No, you don't think me beautiful. I know. Don't worry." She looked directly at the girl. "You are right to ask me that, child. The Witch is said to conjure beauty. It's one of our gifts, one of our powers, did you know? So what happened? Did I simply run out? Is beauty a possession you can run out of? Some would say yes. But if I know the spirits so well and they haven't made me beautiful, why should they make you beautiful?"

No one answered. No one dared to speak a word.

"Yet I have succeeded," she said. "I tell you I have conjured beauty. Don't believe me? Look around!"

She was growing a bit manic, and the crowd was simultaneously enthralled and nervous, as if she were a wild animal that could spring out and strike them. They remembered the lightning and the smell of burning wood. A sense of danger returned.

"All the world is filled with beauty," she said. "You conjure it by truly opening your eyes and seeing what is there for the first time. When you do, beauty is triumphant!

"Be sure to know beauty is not mere prettiness. Beauty can be awesome and terrifying, but still beautiful. True beauty is not safe or tame. And when you open your eyes to true beauty and turn those same eyes upon yourself, you will see how beautiful you really are!"

XVII. Domestication & Wildness

Her wildness did have a beauty, they had to admit. It was as if the villagers could now see her as she truly was for the first time. Her beauty came in the paradox of her wildness and vulnerability. She had to be a creature of magick, for they had come to her door wanting blood, but soon saw a woman, just talking. She had shared her thoughts, feelings, and beliefs, not knowing if they would listen or if they would hurt her. Then her eyes had lit up again, and she was once more a wild creature while still being human. Can it be that we are like this too? they thought.

"Freedom has its price," she said. "We have been domesticated and fenced in. On the one hand, it provides more safety and stability. Nothing wrong with that. On the other, it creates an illusion, the illusion we are safe and stable. Nothing is completely safe and stable. We can only be more or less safe. There are always the blessings and wickedness of fate, of the unseen. Magick can soften the blows, but this is not guaranteed. Nature wants what it wants, even if we do not. To believe otherwise is to lie to yourself and become lazy.

"We seek to be wild. We seek to be free. What is that? Who is absolutely free? Even the wildest of beasts, free to roam, are driven by needs, instinct, and nature. We seek to be independent, yet we are interdependent upon all things.

"We have this romance for freedom, this sense we have lost it and have to regain it at any cost. Yet we don't even know what we are seeking. When we don't understand freedom, we can think we have found it only to realize that we have found loneliness and longing instead. But how we stubbornly cling to our romance of freedom! We often sacrifice happiness for freedom, but we don't have to. No one and no thing can imprison you if you do not choose it. Many beloveds prefer a wild and free experience to the fantasy of domestication you strive for. So look again, who is free?"

The villagers looked from one to the other, certain that one amongst them would cry out, "Here! I am free!" And yet they all stood silently, mouths closed, thoughts swirling.

"The law of the land is hunter and hunted, both, called by their role and nature in the chain," said the Witch. "A hunter to one is the prey of another. The world is not safe, yet it is not unreasonably dangerous. There is a balance between wildness and caution, and you have to find yours, as I've found mine."

She waved her arm, encompassing both the sturdy hut and the wild brambles at her garden gate, the glow of her hearth fire and the shadows slipping like otherworldly otters in the liquid darkness of the forest.

Then she put her hand to her heart, a solid fist against her chest. "And I tell you that you'd best seek it within first. You are the hunter and the hunted. You are what you are seeking. Your true freedom and your safety come from within and when you find them, whatever restricts you in your daily life will not matter, for your heart will be wild and free. The wild beasts are free because they know not. You must be free in your knowing. You must perfect your freedom.

"The wild and free are all around you, invisible and unseen. Those cheering loudly about what wild men and women they are, about how free they are, simply fool themselves. A wild creature will never boast of how free she is."

XVIII.
Faith

The old man shook his head. "You tell us these things, but it's hard to believe it's all true."

"Who is asking you to believe?" the Witch countered. "You ask me these things and I tell you, and now you want me to make you believe? Don't. These are my ideas, based on my experiences and the teachings that have made sense and served me. I'm not here to make my ideas serve you. Take them. Don't. Use them. Don't. I don't care. Find your own experience. Find your own truths. I didn't ask you to adopt all of mine."

The old man's eyes widened. Words failed him. How could she deliver these truths as if they were everything to her, and yet remain so...detached?

Her voice was calm but firm. "You desperately want to believe. After all, I believe. I seem to have no doubts about these things, and you want to be like me, to have no doubts. So you want to have faith in me, in my stories and ideas, and believe.

"Yet I do have doubts, certainly I do. I question my life. I have dark moments that can stretch from days to weeks to months. We all do. But I've explored. I'm free to roam. And this is what works best for now. This is what I think right now. Tomorrow can bring a new experience and revelation. Tomorrow it can all change, and I'm free to change."

"Have you no faith?" he said.

"Faith is the realm of the church. They ask you to put your faith, your belief, in another's experience when they share their story. Believe my story and become like me. It's an important story, they say. A god told it to me, they say, but wait! Not just a god, the God. Now you have to listen. You have to believe because I am not lying, and God can't be wrong. At least not until God tells someone else something different, and then everyone eventually goes to war about it.

"What you are really saying is that it is hard to have faith in me, in what I'm saying. However, I don't ask you to have faith. I ask instead for you to have ideas and experiences. It's said a Witch doesn't believe, a Witch knows. How do we know? Sometimes we remember from other times and lives, but first and foremost, we learn."

He shook his head. "But how? How does one learn these things?"

"Educate yourself. Explore the world. Ask questions. Try things out. Move towards what makes sense. Move towards what brings you fear and upsets you, for where there is fear, there is power. The deepest lessons won't agree with what you already think you know. True seeking requires looking into the unknown and suspending your judgements. True seeking requires you to look into the mirror and see all the good and all the bad. Only by seeing what is can you begin. Only by knowing where you are can you move forward.

"The only faith we have, our true faith, is that which we feel in our bones, in our core. Faith is an unshakable knowledge that, despite being rock steady, is also intangible. If you can define it too clearly, you enter the realm of theology and the Church. Our faith is quite literally the old and unspeakable faith."

XIX.
The Unknown and Unknowable Mysteries

The fire behind her blazed as strongly as ever, yet there was a sense of ending about things. And something more, something shimmering just beyond their collective grasp.

"We are explorers at heart," she said. "We seek the unknown within our own hearts, the unknown within the hearts of others, and the mystery in the heart of nature, the heart of all things.

"Our unspoken faith requires no declarations, as they would be unspeakable, yet our faith constantly tests us. We want to know more about the unknown. So much cannot be put into words, but that doesn't mean we don't still try. And we fail. And we try some more. And when we succeed, even if only in part, we open the door to understanding.

"We are always pointed in the direction of the unknown, of the mystery, yet there will always be aspects unknowable to us in one lifetime. We won't even know to ask the question let alone seek the answer, but that should not stop us from asking the questions. The greatest question of the Mysteries—beyond the questions of all people, such as 'Who am I? Why am I here? What happens next?'—is the question of all initiates in the Mysteries: How do I serve?"

XX.
Power

"Serve who?" the old farmer demanded. "All this talk of what we have to do for ourselves and now you want us to serve other people? That sounds very much like church talk to me."

The people waited. It was a question they had been thinking amongst themselves, after all. They had been taught to serve, yes, always someone higher and stronger, someone with more power, whether king or commander or god. The old woman had opened a crack in that wall of requirement. And now she was leading them back to the way they had always lived?

The Witch saw their confusion. "Do not misunderstand. We should seek power in order to serve, yes, but to serve the All, you must first learn to serve yourself. If you are not able to serve yourself, then you will be useless in the long run to give to others, yet we have learned to see self-sacrifice and martyrdom as glorious. You see it nowhere else in nature, and when you leave nature, you see the imbalance of humanity, with good intentions as well as ill.

"First you must care for your own needs. Then you must explore your desires. If done with good will, the desires that serve and satisfy will lead to your soul's purpose, and the ones that do not can be exorcised by dissatisfaction, like unwanted spirits. Holy desire will lead you to your souls, to your true power.

"Fear can be a barrier to—and a teacher of—true power. Our fear contains a lot of our power. When we reject our power because we are unsure of what to do with it, we give it over to fear. Like a friend, fear holds onto it for us. When we get upset with fear for keeping us from our power, just as we asked it to do, we grow angry and resentful. We think we are reclaiming our power, and we do find power of a sort, but fear keeps holding true power. This can lead to jealousy, shame, and grief. Only when we face fear directly do we regain our true power, because our true power can never leave us, it just goes unused when we don't realize it."

She stepped forward, and it was as if she were aflame with invisible fire. There was solidness to her, deep like tree roots, but also an openness, wide like the sky at the top of the mountain. And the villagers felt it one by one like a wave, a stirring in the blood, a spark igniting.

"True power is not power over others, over armies and nations," she said, "but power to be in alignment with your inner nation. Kings and leaders can create much chaos and do much good from their position, yet few have found true power. Still a beggar in the street in true power can move mountains with a word. Unseen chain reactions occur with every thought, word, and deed of one who is aligned with true power. Often the results will not be known in their lifetime, as each result is the cause of a new event, a chain of experience. It's true of us all, though those in their power do more with less effort and are the makers of miracles, while those simply in positions of power must harness the great efforts of the masses with reward or manipulation.

"Those in their true power are the secret sovereigns of their own nation of selfhood and in many ways are the true leaders of this world. At one time our tribal and national kings and queens could be counted among them, understanding the balance and fulfilling the sacred pacts, but no more. Now it is up to each and every one of us to be our own secret sovereign and gently guide the fate of the world by our thoughts, words, and deeds."

XXI.
Love

"What about love?" a young woman said.

She had been previously silent, as had her husband. They were young, newly wedded and struggling in this lean time, but hope ran through them both like the green current of life in a spring sapling. They stood shoulder to shoulder now.

"Yes," her husband said, "you have forgotten love. We are commanded to love, and that is more important that power."

The Witch remembered the young wife. She had come to that very hut, and the Witch had brewed teas for her to heal and nurture the child that grew within her.

"Many seek love before or instead of seeking power," she said, "not realizing that love is a holy desire to be fulfilled. Like true power, true love is deeply misunderstood.

"At first, love is equated with approval. We learn this from our parents even when they try not to teach it because we are rewarded for certain behaviors and reprimanded for others. We soon equate reward for love and believe we will only be loved if we behave in a way that is approved. To do otherwise is to risk losing love."

The young wife blushed. She had brought those same worries to the Witch, having learned them from her father and mother.

The Witch saw her eyes keen with growing knowledge. "When we risk love in one place, we seek others who approve, who validate what we are doing. We then feel justified and vindicated even if we have lost love.

"Love becomes the romantic ideal. We seek love of self in another, but like freedom, if we don't find it within, no one else can help us find it. Lovers and spouses can share their love with us. They can show their love, but they can't make you believe it or feel it.

"We explore all the confusing permutations of love. There are differences between the love between spouses and the love we show towards children. We love our parents differently than our friends. Bonds are formed in groups and under trials of combat that are deeply loving. They are all different, but they are all love. And they all require us to truly love ourselves."

The young husband's arm went around his wife's waist, protectively, assuredly. She accepted his gesture of protection even as she stood straight and firm on her own two feet, one hand on her belly.

The Witch's voice was gentle but strong. "Remember, love does not own. You do. Love does not possess anyone, nor can anyone possess you. You can only possess yourself and choose to share your heart. People are not playthings to be used and discarded, or worse yet, saved and hidden away so no other may find them.

"As we mature, we seek reconciliation. We recognize at least intellectually that love is not based in our behavior, and we seek out those who we believe have rejected us and those we have rejected and seek to make amends. We give and we accept forgiveness, and in doing so, find a new level of love.

"Along the way to reconciliation, we seek to learn empathy. Many are empathic, feeling overwhelmed with the feelings of others, but few learn to relate to others and develop true empathy. Along the way we might learn pity, to seemingly empathize while still feeling superior. Only when we relate as equals, having the same inherent worth despite our differences, will we gain compassion and seek to alleviate suffering."

The villagers listened and remembered. Not all of them knew the kind of love she was talking about, but they all knew suffering. Suffering came to everyone. Supposedly that was their due, according to the minister, in this vale of tears. But this old woman was saying something more complicated, something harder and yet more hopeful at the same time.

"From compassion we gain understanding of unconditional love, true love, perfect love," the Witch said. "This is the love of the sages and mystics, this is the love of saints and gods. We soon realize this is the love of unconditional interconnectedness. It is that which binds us together, the esoteric magnets of the universe available to all, every moment of every day. We have simply forgotten. Yet we have always belonged. There has always been a place for us. We have always had meaning and purpose even when we and others fail to see it. That is true love."

XXII.
Wisdom

The conversation had taken an unexpected turn. A witch talking deeply about love? Wasn't it all about attraction spells and lust potions? And now wisdom? She sounded like a philosopher.

The Witch still stood in her doorway, but the fire behind her was low now, a glow of golden coals. The shadows around her were no longer black and dense—they were the gray of spiderwebbing, velvet and gossamer.

"Wisdom is knowing how to express your power, or your thought," she said. "Wisdom is knowing when to take action and when to be still. Wisdom is knowing when to show mercy, when to forgive and forget, and when to hold a boundary or ask for more. Not knowing the difference is foolishness, as there is a time and place for both.

"Wisdom is seeking knowledge in the world around you, from everywhere and everyone. Never assume you are wiser than another until they prove it to be true, and even then doubt, as the wisest often play the role of the fool and some fools appears to be wise. Look to the plants, to the animals, and to the stones. Turn over every rock for its mystery. Seek the wisdom of the stars. Listen to your body. Listen to others. Listen. The wise listen more than they speak.

"Wisdom is the reconciliation of paradox in your heart, knowing it will never be completely clear in your mind and yet making peace with it. Reconciliation leads to that unspeakable faith we know in our bones."

The villagers listened, their minds teeming. Yes, they could feel something in their bones, but it felt more like weariness now. The storm has passed. A freshness followed even if the landscape was strewn with leaves and branches, riots of chaos here and there. And the barn! They had forgotten about the barn. There would be work in the morning. But then they looked around, and the understanding crept up, slow and steady and inexorable...the morning was already upon them.

The Witch saw their realization, and her mouth curved in what might have been a smile. "You are not unique. Not special. Yet there has never been anyone like you before and there never will be again. Remember this always."

And with that, the Witch turned, looked across the crowd for a moment over her shoulder, and then entered her hut, slamming the door and leaving her spellbound audience wet as a new day began to dawn in the gray east. One by one, they turned and went back to their village, no longer a mob. They had no choice but to go home and think about what they learned at the hut that night.

And so they did.

Afterword

I began this book as a catharsis. I had a conflict with a personality in the Witchcraft world and was really dwelling on the concept of blame and victimhood, and how many of us on the Witch's path have this persecution complex where we need to blame the other, even as the history of the Witch has been the role of the "other" taking the blame, real or exaggerated, and becoming a scapegoat for society's ills. We need to understand and transform this pattern, as modern Witches.

I was asking a lot of questions about why things happened the way they do and why people behave as they do. I thought I was just asking myself, not in any formal meditative or ritual way, not expecting an answer, but my answers started coming in the form of the voice, the Witch, from this story. I felt compelled to write it.

It was around the winter holidays of 2014, and I was feeling a bit wistful for my departed mother. One of her favorite books is Khalil Gibran's *The Prophet*. I had been reading it at the previous Samhain holiday and soon realized in some ways this story was a tip of the hat to that masterpiece. Then suddenly it stopped. Nothing more flowed. The Witch's voice grew silent. We made amends, the famous personality and I, though since then we have had our last and final falling out, and I continued onward with other writing and teaching projects.

When I found myself questioning, or in conflict, the Witch's voice came back. The story would continue. Sometimes I would only get out a few lines. Other times it would be a whole short chapter. It only flowed when I was facing things she could answer, and it sometimes led me in some strange directions. Soon it built momentum, but still I could only do little bits at a time. So I was doing little bits every day. Some of the lore came as things I knew, wisdom I was taught or read. I recognized some of the words and teachings from favorite authors, elders, peers, and friends, but they came out in different ways. Other ideas were new to me, for even as I wrote, the Witch was teaching me too.

I thought of the Witch in the hut as a spirit, but I've never seen her in a meditation or vision. I've never encountered her in a dream. Just here in my head, as I wrote in the dark night when everyone else was asleep. I have guesses on who she might be, if anyone at all, but they are only guesses, nothing concrete or clear, just hints of intuition. The messenger is less important than the message, something I often have to remind myself.

Isn't that the path though? She reminded me of things I knew, but had forgotten. She gave new interpretative twists to those things, and sometimes even a brand new understanding. I've still never seen her in meditation, vision, or dream, but this is how it works to walk the Crooked Path—you never get what you expect.

About the Author

An award-winning author, Christopher Penczak is also a teacher and healing practitioner. As an advocate for the timeless wisdom of the ages, he is rooted firmly in the traditions of modern witchcraft and Earth-based religions, but draws from a wide range of spiritual traditions including shamanism, alchemy, herbalism, Theosophy and Hermetic Qabalah to forge his own magickal path.

Christopher is the author of over two dozen books on various aspects of Witchcraft, the occult, and spiritual practice, including *The Temple of Witchcraft* series, *The Mystic Foundation,* and *The Phosphorous Grove.*

www.ingramcontent.com/pod-product-compliance
Lightning Source LLC
Chambersburg PA
CBHW031359160426
42813CB00094B/3465/J